Forex For Beginners

Learn How To Get Rich Forex Trading For Beginners

Table of Contents

Introduction

Forex is the learning and art of exchanging distinctive monetary standards and making benefit through it. You realize that every nation has its own particular money, and the currency of distinctive nations can be purchased and sold against one another. Forex traders are those individuals who profit through purchasing and offering diverse monetary forms against one another. Forex is not another business, and its history is as old as the historical backdrop of cash.

There are individuals who have been profiting through Forex from numerous years back. Luckily, with the assistance of the personal computer and internet, Forex trading has turned out to be much simpler. You can sit at your PC and exchange from home without needing to make any telephone call or alluding to any bank. The way that we exchange forex, and through the exchanging framework that we have added to, an expert forex dealer needs to spend just 30 minutes for every day, to find the exchanging open doors and take his positions. At that point he can go and make the most of his life, and return tomorrow.

There are business organizations that empower you to purchase and offer diverse monetary forms through the Internet and some basic virtual products that are called exchanging stages. For any exchange that you make, you pay a little commission to the financier organization that you are exchanging through. You have to locate a decent, dependable and understood business organization and sign up for a record with it. At that point you need to finance your record. You utilize the cash you have in your record to exchange. Any benefit that you make, will be added to your record and vice versa. At that point you can pull back the cash you have made.

Chapter 1 – What Is Forex Trading?

Forex is a regularly utilized shortened form for "foreign exchange". It normally depicts the purchasing and offering of cash in the foreign exchange market, particularly by financial specialists. The natural expression that purchase low and offer high, surely applies to cash exchanging. A forex broker buys monetary standards that are underestimated and offers currency that is exaggerated; generally as a stock dealer buys stock that is underestimated and offers stock that is also exaggerated.

There is a wide variety of dealers in the foreign exchange market.

The most essential among them are the banks. Banks managing in foreign exchange have branches with significant equalizations in many countries and among many nations. Through their branches, the administrations of such banks, normally called Exchange Banks, are accessible everywhere throughout the world.

These banks markdown and offer foreign bills of exchange, issue bank drafts, impact telegraphic exchanges and other credit instruments, and rebate and gather sums on the premise of such records. Different dealers in foreign exchange are bill agents who help venders and purchasers in foreign bills to meet up.

Service houses is another class of dealers in foreign exchange. They help impact on foreign settlements by tolerating bills for the benefit of clients. The national bank and treasury of a nation are additionally dealers in foreign exchange. Both may mediate in the market infrequently. Today, in any case, these powers oversee exchange rates and execute exchange controls in different ways.

Functions of forex

Following are the functions associated with forex market:

To exchange fund, buying force starting with one country then onto the next. Such exchange is influenced through foreign bills or settlements made through telegraphic exchange.

To make procurement for supporting offices, like, to encourage purchasing and offering spot or forward foreign exchange.

Transfer functions

The essential capacity of the foreign exchange market is to encourage the change of one coin into another, i.e., to finish exchanges of buying force between two nations. This exchange of buying force is affected through a mixed bag of acknowledge instruments, for example, telegraphic exchanges, bank draft and foreign bills.

In performing the exchange work, the foreign exchange market completes installments universally by clearing obligations in both headings all the while, similar to household clearings.

Credit function

Another capacity of the foreign exchange market is to give credit, both national and global, to advance foreign exchange. Clearly, when foreign bills of exchange are utilized as a part of universal installments, a credit for around 3 months, till their development is needed.

Hedging function

A third capacity of the foreign exchange market is to support foreign exchange hazards. Hedging means the evasion of a foreign exchange hazard. In a free exchange market when exchange rate, which is the cost of one cash regarding another money, change, there may be an increase or misfortune to the gathering concerned. Under this condition, a man or a firm attempts an extraordinary exchange hazard if there are immense measures of net claims or net liabilities which are to be met in foreign cash.

Exchange hazard in that capacity ought to be stayed away from or decreased. For this, the exchange market gives offices to hedging foreseen or real claims or liabilities through forward contracts. A forward contract, which is typically for three months, is an agreement to purchase or offer foreign exchange against another money at some altered date later on at a cost settled upon now.

No cash gets relaxation as per the agreement. But, the agreement makes it conceivable to disregard any probable changes in exchange rate. The presence of a forward market in this way makes it conceivable to fence an exchange position.

Foreign bills of exchange, telegraphic exchange, bank draft, letter of credit, and so on, are the essential foreign exchange instruments utilized as a part of the foreign exchange market to complete its capacities.

Cautions for dealing in forex

If you want to exchange cash sets in the Forex Markets, the accompanying cautions are demonstrated as follows. Be mindful so as to evade Forex tricks. Unfortunately, there are numerous of them which should be avoided by you.

When you open a Forex record, it is not important to have your cash as a safe money with contributor protection. It is not important for opening a fates account where your cash is ensured in view of the exchange's imprint to-market rules. You basically need to pick a legitimate firm or you could lose your exchanging record. Believe it or not, you could lose each penny. Such misfortune has effectively happened when Forex dealers have gone belly up. So it's dependent upon you to pick a decent agent.

Since the time that retail Forex started, it is fundamental that you work with respectable Forex specialists from the country that requests high industry guidelines for Forex firms.

Then again, the U.S. has tight industry norms and the strictest regulation for Forex firms. So does Canada, the U.K., Australia and Hong Kong. So if you have your record domiciled with any of these countries, you're as of now on top of things. Yet, past that you likewise need to locate a respectable and very much promoted firm inside of your nature of decision.

- Place your well-deserved money just with a firm that is exceptionally managed and is very much promoted. These two focuses are critical.
- Truth should be told at any cost to get right information about data used in trading.
-

Forex dealers are not so much honest. They bait individuals in with buildup and false publicizing. Who in his right personality is going to need to exchange 24 hours unless he has an uncommon need? While the reality of the matter is that aggregate Forex volume is more noteworthy than in the prospects, fates volume at the exchange is more noteworthy than the volume at a Forex dealer for the most prominently exchanged monetary forms.

What most brokers don't understand is that the lion's share of Forex volume is exchanged specifically in the middle of banks, and that incredible volume is never seen at the retail trader level. The main spot where the liquidity differential matters is in monetary standards like the Mexican peso, the Brazilian genuine, and some individual's krone. Those meagerly exchanged monetary forms may be more fluid in Forex. But, if you exchange anything other than the couple of most fluid and prevalent monetary standards, you will be paying no less than 5 pips, and regularly more. Unless you have a specific business need to arrangement in Polish zlotys, Indian rupees, or some other daintily exchanged coin, you needn't bother with Forex.

Likely you have heard that if you win frequently in Forex, you may be banished from exchanging. Is this genuine? Yes, it is true. The way that it is genuine is simply one more verification that when you exchange Forex, you are exchanging at a container shop. In the book, "Memories of a Stock Operator," you are informed that Jesse Livermore was banned from exchanging at certain stock specialists on the grounds that they couldn't stand his beating the house. The same thing is valid with numerous Forex intermediaries. Since they are the ones ensuring you a fill, they are as a result the purchaser and trader of final resort. The fact of the matter is that most Forex specialists have valuable little liquidity at their organizations.

Keeping in mind the end goal to give you the feeling that there is liquidity, it is the trader who gives you your fill. It is the trader who does the quit running that as far as anyone knows doesn't exist in Forex. However, if you are routinely beating the socks off the trader, he will restrict you from exchanging at his firm. This can happen notwithstanding when the trader cases to not have an arrangement work area.

Chapter 2 – The Significance of Forex Trading

The foreign exchange market is the world's greatest money related market by a long shot. As indicated by the Bank for International Settlement's triennial overview, worldwide forex turnover in April 2010 arrived at the midpoint of an amazing $4.0 trillion every day, an increment of 20% from $3.3 trillion three years prior.

In an undeniably globalized economy, the importance of the foreign exchange marketplace to the normal shopper can't be thought little of. The rate at which the local cash can be exchanged in the worldwide forex market decides the cost you pay for an expanding number of items, the sticker for your excursions, the rate of profit for your ventures and even the premium rate on your advances and stores.

But then, notwithstanding the significance of this market, where money gyrations can manage the fortunes of everybody from the biggest country to the littlest shoppers, foreign exchange remains to a great extent, an unregulated business. Albeit foreign exchange has generally been viewed as the restrictive area of the greatest banks and enterprises, late patterns have scattered this idea, making it progressively essential for foreign exchange to go under the heading of regulation.

Institutional investors

On the institutional side, where national banks freely manage their coin markets. Notwithstanding, no single worldwide controller exists to control the overall forex market. In any case, the institutional forex market additionally needs regulation for various reasons, including:

Higher Hedging Costs

Increased money unpredictability brought on by unnecessary theory prompts higher expenses acquired by partnerships and other business players for hedging cash hazard.

Systemic Importance of Big Banks

While forex exchanging misfortunes were not conspicuous in the greatest exchanging misfortunes posted by enterprises and budgetary establishments to date, the potential does exist for billion-dollar misfortunes on wrong coin wagers. In spite of the fact that money exchanging is a zero-entirety diversion, an enormous misfortune acquired by a major bank could have an expansive influence on the worldwide economy because of its systemic significance.

Importance of Forex

The forex market is the foundation of worldwide exchange and worldwide contributing in foreign exchange. It is discriminating to bolster imports and exports, which are important to obtain entrance to assets and to make extra interest for products and administrations. Without the capacity to exchange distinctive monetary forms, organizations' prospects would be constrained and worldwide financial development would endure.

Speculators likewise utilize the forex market. The individuals who look for worldwide expansion advantages need to exchange currency to purchase and offer foreign resources and securities. A few speculators view monetary forms as an advantage class and exchange currency to produce alpha.

Monetary forms are exchanged electronically and reciprocally over the counter. One test for financial specialists is to recognize, where the market is, the point at which they need to exchange in view of constrained straightforwardness about forex exchanges.

Forex Fixing and Its Importance?

Restricted straightforwardness about exchanges joined with the way that forex rates influence such a large number of exchanges means there is a requirement for some kind of a benchmark, that is, a solitary rate that mirrors the estimation of one cash in respect to others at a specific point in time. This benchmark is known as a fix.

While there are numerous forex fixes, the primary ones are resolved in London at 11am and 4pm consistently. A forex fix is ordinarily made from a preview of real exchanges inside of a tight window of time, say 30 seconds, not at all like Libor that depends on assessed rates. In any case, concerns have emerged that controlled exchanging around the fix's season may misshape the determination of the forex rate benchmark.

It makes a difference as a result of the pervasive part of forex fixes. These rates are utilized by organizations, speculators and resource administrators. Forex rates are important to esteem resources, liabilities and a substantial number of exchanges for products and administrations named in distinctive monetary forms. A few financial specialists even exchange on the fix, training their dealer to purchase or offer a sure measure of money at the 4pm fix.

Forex rates likewise frame the premise for execution assessment and danger administration. For instance, they are utilized for hedging against money changes to oversee danger and they can be utilized to estimate by expecting danger with the trust of acquiring an arrival.

Chapter 3 – Forex Trading Tips and Strategies

The foreign exchange market is a worldwide decentralized marketplace that decides the relative estimations of distinctive monetary standards. Dissimilar to different markets, there is no concentrated safe or exchange where exchanges are led. Rather, these exchanges are led by a few market members in a few areas. It is uncommon that any two coinage will be indistinguishable to each other in worth, and it's likewise uncommon that any two monetary standards will keep up the same relative quality for more than a brief time of time. In forex, the exchange rate between two monetary forms always shows signs of change.

Regarding the matter of selecting techniques to exchange, you have the decision between purchasing coincidental the-rack and trawling the Internet for freebies. The issue with free forex exchanging systems is that they are generally worth about as much as you pay for them. They haven't been tried, and there is little proof of their dependability.

Not the accompanying's majority procedures are equivalent in all markets. Some perform superior to anything others, and every individual trader will discover a few procedures more suitable for them to exchange than others.

- The Blade runner is a particularly decent EMA hybrid technique, suitable over all time periods and money sets. It is an inclining technique that tries to pick breakouts from a continuation and exchange the retests.

- Fibonacci Pivot Trades join Fibonacci retracements and expansions with day by day, week by week, month to month and even yearly turns. The accentuation in the examination here is on utilizing these blends with every day rotates just, however the thought can without much of a stretch be reached out to longer time periods consolidating any mix of turns.
- The Bolly Band Bounce Trade is immaculate in an extending market. Numerous traders use it in blend with affirming signs, to awesome impact. If Bollinger Bands engage you, this one is definitely justified even despite a look.

- The Dual Stochastic Trade clients two stochastics, one moderate and one quick, in mix to pick territories where cost is drifting however overextended in a transient retracement, and going to snap once again into a pattern's continuation.
- Overlapping Fibonacci exchanges are the top picks of a few dealers I have known. If utilized naturally, their unwavering quality can be a bit lower than a percentage of alternate methodologies, however if you utilize them in conjunction with suitable affirming signs, they can be to a great degree precise.

- The additional instability you get when London

opens introduces some one of a kind open doors. The London Hammer Trade is my interpretation of an endeavor to exploit these open doors. Particularly powerful amid the London session, it can be utilized whenever when cost is liable to be taking off unequivocally in one bearing, and perhaps turning around from a territory of bolster/resistance pretty much as firmly.

- As specified over, the Blade runner is a pattern taking after method. The Blade runner inversion pretty much as adequately picks passages from circumstances where the pattern switches and value starts to exchange on the opposite side of the EMA's.
- If you've ever attempted to pursue cost when it limits

away to the upside, just to endure the inescapable misfortune when it pretty much as fast inverts, you will need the pop's mystery and stop exchange your broker's stockpile. There is a basic trap to figuring out if or not cost will proceed toward the breakout, and you must know it keeping in mind the end goal to benefit from these circumstances.

- The flip side of the pop and stop, this methodology exchanges savage breakouts to the drawback.
- The forex fractal is a methodology as well as an idea of market basics that you truly need to know keeping in mind the end goal to comprehend what cost is doing, why it is doing it, and who is making it move. This is the sort of inside data that

took me years and numerous a large number of dollars to learn. It's yours here for nothing, so make utilization of it.

There are likewise a few locales offering free methodologies. The issue with a large portion of these locales is, as said above, they simply give a brief portrayal of every technique, with minimal genuine evidence that they work. Hence, there is a requirement for more prominent exploration on your part before utilizing any of those procedures as a part of your genuine exchanging. When you have chosen a procedure from one of these sources you will obviously need to altogether back test and forward test it.

The different procedures for this are secured in Forex Strategy Testing There are additionally a few business frameworks to consider. Since these are more extensive than the basic techniques displayed above, and in this way fall into the meaning of Forex Trading System, they are managed independently in the accompanying segment, Forex Trading Systems

Chapter 4 – The Simplicity Of Making Money Through Forex

In the forex market, you actually purchase or offer currencies.

Setting an exchange the foreign exchange market is straightforward: the mechanics of an exchange are fundamentally the same to those found in different markets (like the share trading system), so if you have any involvement in exchanging, you ought to have the capacity to lift it up before long.

The objective of forex is to exchange one cash for another in the desire that the cost will change, so that the currency you purchased will increment in quality contrasted with the one you sold.

For example:

Trader's Action	
You purchase 10,000 euros at the EUR/USD exchange rate of **1.1800**	+1
Two weeks later, you exchange your 10,000 euros back into U.S. dollar at the exchange rate of **1.2500**	-1
You earn a profit of **$700**	

*EUR 10,000 x 1.18 = US $11,800

** EUR 10,000 x 1.25 = US $12,500

An exchange rate is just the proportion of one money esteemed against another cash. For instance, the USD/CHF exchange rate shows what number of U.S. dollars can buy one Swiss franc, or what number of Swiss francs you have to purchase one U.S. dollar.

Reading the forex code

Monetary forms are constantly cited in sets or pairs, for example, GBP/USD or USD/JPY. The reason they are cited in sets is on the grounds that in each foreign exchange, you are at the same time purchasing one money and offering another. Here is a sample of a foreign exchange rate for the British pound versus the U.S. dollar:

GBP/USD forex quote

The initially recorded coin to one side of the slash is known as the base money (in this illustration it is the British pound), while the second one on the privilege is known as the counter or quote cash (in this sample, the U.S. dollar).

At the point when purchasing, the exchange rate lets you know the amount you need to pay in units of the quote money to purchase one unit of the base cash. In the illustration above, you need to pay 1.51258 U.S. dollars to purchase 1 British pound.

At the point when offering, the exchange rate lets you know what number of units of the quote cash you get for offering one unit of the base coin. In the sample above, you will get 1.51258 U.S. dollars when you offer 1 British pound.

The base money is the premise for the purchase or the offer. If you purchase EUR/USD this essentially implies that you are purchasing the base coin and all the while offering the quote money. In Stone Age man talk, purchase EUR, offer USD.

You would purchase the pair if you trust the base money will acknowledge (increase esteem) with respect to the quote coin. You would offer the pair if you think the base cash will devalue (lose esteem) with respect to the quote money.

Long and short selling

To start with, you ought to figure out if you need to purchase or offer.

If you need to purchase (which really means purchase the base cash and offer the quote money), you need the base coin to ascend in worth and afterward you would offer it back at a higher cost. In broker's discussion, this is called going long or taking a long position. Just recollect: long = purchase.

If you need to offer which really means offer the base money and purchase the quote cash, you need the base coin to fall in worth and afterward you would purchase it back at a lower cost. This is called going short or taking a short position.

Bid and ask rate

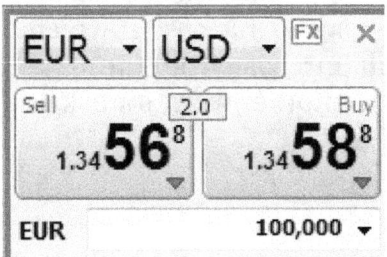

All forex quotes are cited with two costs: the offer and inquire. Generally, the offer is lower than the ask cost.

The offer is the cost at which your intermediary is willing to purchase the base coin in exchange for the quote cash. This implies the offer is the best accessible cost at which you (the dealer) will offer to the market.

The ask rate is the cost at which your trader will offer the base money in exchange for the quote cash. This implies the ask cost is the best accessible cost at which you will purchase from the market. Another word for ask is the offer cost.

Chapter 5 – Easy Strategies For Improving Your Forex Trading

Whether you're new to Currency Trading or a prepared broker, you can simply enhance your exchanging abilities. Training is major to fruitful exchanging. Here are six stages that will help sharpen your Currency exchanging abilities.

Fruitful expert dealers do three things that novices frequently overlook. They arrange an exchanging methodology, they take after the markets, and they diarize, track, and investigate each of their exchanges.

Plan How You Will Trade

You may have heard the maxim, if you neglect to arrange, you plan to fizzle. This is especially valid in Forex hypothesis. Effective brokers begin with a sound method and they stick to it at all times.

Pick the coin matches that are a good fit for you

Some coin sets are unstable and move a ton intra-day. Some coin sets are unfaltering and make moderate moves over longer time periods. In view of your danger parameters, choose which money sets are most appropriate to your exchanging procedure.

Choose to what extent you plan to stay in a position

In light of your cash pair choice, arrangement to what extent you need to hold your positions: minutes, hours, or days. Keep in mind that relying upon your record sort, having open positions at 5:00pm Eastern Time may bring about rollover charges.

Set your objectives for the position

Before you take a position you ought to build up your way out methodology. If the position is a victor, at what rate will you money out? If the position is a failure, at what rate will you cut your misfortunes? At that point, put your stops and breaking points appropriately.

Take after the Forex Market

Use Forex graphs and Forex news to screen market data and specialized levels that influence your positions.

Use Forex Charts

Diagrams are a crucial instrument to enhance exchanging returns. You can without much of a stretch recover the cash spent on a diagramming bundle from a solitary all around put exchange in view of the investigation from expert graphs. Look at XE Charts. It would be ideal if you remember that forex exchanging includes a high danger of misfortune, and no insurance is made that the venture on the outlining applications will be recovered.

Take after Forex News

Forex News gives breaking Forex news on monetary reports and political occasions that impact the coin market. You can get to nitty gritty market analysis and exchanging procedures from experienced Forex dealers.

Keep a Forex Diary

Most traders fall flat in light of the fact that they commit the same errors again and again. A journal can help by staying informed regarding what lives up to expectations for you and what doesn't. Utilized reliably, a well-kept journal is your closest companion. At the point when keeping your journal, verify that it contains in any event the accompanying:

- The date and time you took the position.
- The rate at which you took the position.
- The reason you took the position.
- Your method for the position.
- The date and time you left the position.
- The rate at which you left the position.
- Your benefit/misfortune on the position.

When you figure out how to perceive fruitful exchanging examples, you will have the capacity to spot them when they return. Be mindful that exchanging foreign exchange on edge conveys an abnormal state of danger, and may not be suitable for all financial specialists. The high level of influence can conflict with you and additionally for you. Before choosing to put resources into foreign exchange you ought to precisely consider your venture goals, level of experience, and danger longing.

The likelihood exists that you could manage a loss of some or the greater part of your beginning speculation and thusly you ought not to contribute cash that you can't bear to lose. You ought to be mindful of the considerable number of dangers connected with foreign exchange exchanging, and look for exhortation from an autonomous monetary counselor if you have any questions.

Breaking point Orders

A breaking point request educates the framework to consequently leave a position when your objective benefit has been accomplished. This empowers you to secure your sought benefit on a triumphant position.

Stop/Loss Orders

A stop/misfortune request teaches the framework to consequently leave a position when the most extreme misfortune farthest point has been hit. This empowers you to top your misfortunes on a losing position.

Exchanging Discipline

Proficient Traders utilization Limit Orders and Stop/Loss Orders as the foundation of a trained exchanging technique. By setting both on every one of their positions, they have expelled feeling from the mathematical statement and are letting the market work for them.

Beginners, then again, don't utilization Limit Orders and Stop/Loss Orders. They stay stuck to their screens, attempting to juggle every one of their positions progressively. They miss basic activity focuses, and they let feeling control their choices.

Setting Limit and Stop/Loss Orders
When in doubt of thumb, you your Stop/Loss Orders ought to be set closer to the opening position cost than your Limit Orders. If you do this, then you can be fruitful while being correct under half of the time.

For instance, if you utilize a 100 pip Limit Order with a 30 pip Stop/Loss Order on every one of your positions, then you just to be correct 1/3 of the opportunity to make a benefit.

Where you put your Limit and Stop/Loss Orders will rely on upon your danger resistance. On the other hand, you should be keen when setting them. If a Stop/Loss Order is excessively near the opening position value, it can be activated by ordinary market instability. This implies that an impermanent plunge can thump out a position before it has an opportunity to follow. Correspondingly, if a Limit Order is set to a long way from the opening value, potential benefit might never be figured it out.

Be mindful that exchanging foreign exchange on edge conveys an abnormal state of danger, and may not be suitable for all financial specialists. The high level of influence can conflict with

you and in addition for you.
Before choosing to put resources
into foreign exchange you ought
to painstakingly consider your
venture targets, level of
experience, and danger craving.
The likelihood exists that you
could maintain a loss of some or
the majority of your starting
venture and accordingly you
ought not to contribute cash that
you can't bear to lose.

Brokers utilizing Technical
Analysis take after graphs and
patterns, regularly taking after a
number money matches at the
same time. Brokers utilizing
Fundamental Analysis must deal
with a lot of market information,
thus commonly concentrate on
just a couple money sets.
Therefore, numerous brokers
lean toward Technical Analysis.

Moreover, numerous traders pick Technical Analysis in light of the fact that they see solid drifting inclinations in the Forex market. They hope to ace the essentials of Technical Analysis and apply them to various time periods and coin sets.

Be mindful that exchanging foreign exchange on edge conveys an abnormal state of danger, and may not be suitable for all financial specialists. The high level of influence can conflict with you and also for you. Before choosing to put resources into foreign exchange you ought to deliberately consider your speculation goals, level of experience, and danger voracity. The likelihood exists that you could manage a loss of some or the majority of your introductory venture and subsequently you ought not to contribute cash that you can't stand to lose.

Conclusion

Thank you again for downloading this book!

The foreign exchange market is a spot where foreign funds are purchased and sold. Foreign exchange market is an institutional course of action for purchasing and offering of foreign monetary forms. Exporter offers the foreign monetary forms and traders purchase them. It is simply a cash market with main focus on money. The purchasers and dealers of foreign cash with the buyers and sellers together constitute a foreign exchange market. It is not confined to any given nation or a topographical region. Along these lines, the foreign exchange market is the market for a foreign cash for anyplace on the planet, as the money related terms of the world are united in a solitary market.

Forex is an online home based business that needn't bother with showcasing, selecting and promoting. You just manage the monetary standards through the Internet. So you won't need to answer any email, make any telephone call and spend any cash on publicizing, or manage the clients, customers, members, supporters and referrals. You don't need to ship anything to any purchaser. You don't need to be agonized over rivalry in your Forex business, in light of the fact that around here you don't contend with anyone.

www.ingramcontent.com/pod-product-compliance
Lightning Source LLC
Chambersburg PA
CBHW070406190526
45169CB00003B/1132